Bocce

Evangelene Alaraj

Backyard Games

AV2

Step 1
Go to **www.openlightbox.com**

Step 2
Enter this unique code

SPOCBFRUM

Step 3
Explore your interactive eBook!

CONTENTS

AV2 is optimized for use on any device

Your interactive eBook comes with...

Contents
Browse a live contents page to easily navigate through resources

Audio
Listen to sections of the book read aloud

Videos
Watch informative video clips

Weblinks
Gain additional information for research

Slideshows
View images and captions

Try This!
Complete activities and hands-on experiments

Key Words
Study vocabulary, and complete a matching word activity

Quizzes
Test your knowledge

Share
Share titles within your Learning Management System (LMS) or Library Circulation System

Citation
Create bibliographical references following the Chicago Manual of Style

This title is part of our AV2 digital subscription

1-Year 3–8 Subscription
ISBN 978-1-7911-3306-1

Access hundreds of AV2 titles with our digital subscription.
Sign up for a FREE trial at **www.openlightbox.com/trial**

Backyard Games

BOCCE

CONTENTS

What Is Bocce?

Sunshine often makes people want to get outside and enjoy the weather. Fun can happen anywhere, even in the backyard. The backyard is a great place to gather and play games.

Bocce is a popular backyard game. Two teams roll or toss eight balls toward a small target ball, called the pallino. Points go to the team whose ball is closest to the pallino. Play continues for several rounds. The first team to get 12 points wins.

Ancient Egyptian paintings suggest that games similar to bocce have been played for thousands of years. Italians developed the game into what it is today. The word "bocce" comes from the Latin word *bottia*, meaning "ball."

Some countries have their own **versions** of bocce. The British call their version lawn bowls. Several differences in rules or equipment make each style unique. In all styles, the main goal is to get as close as possible to the target ball.

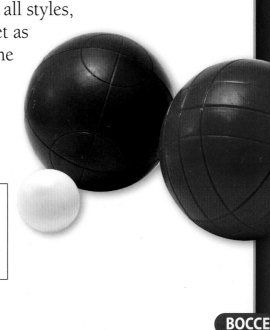

The pallino is generally white. This ball is also known as the jack or *cochonnet*, which means "piglet" in French.

Timeline

Bocce was popular in ancient times and remains so to this day. It has been played to pass the time and as friendly competition.

Egyptian wall paintings and vases show young people playing a bowling game with small balls.

5200 BC

1ST TO 5TH CENTURY AD

14TH TO 16TH CENTURY

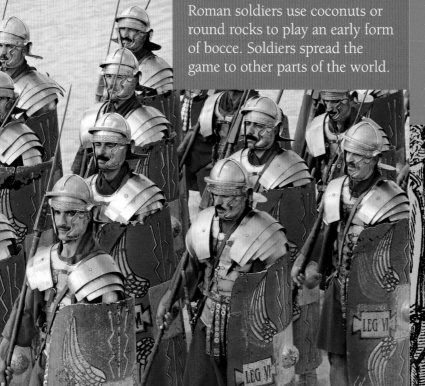

Roman soldiers use coconuts or round rocks to play an early form of bocce. Soldiers spread the game to other parts of the world.

European kings **ban** bocce. France's King Charles IV bans it in 1319. In England, King Henry VIII allows commoners to play only on Christmas Day.

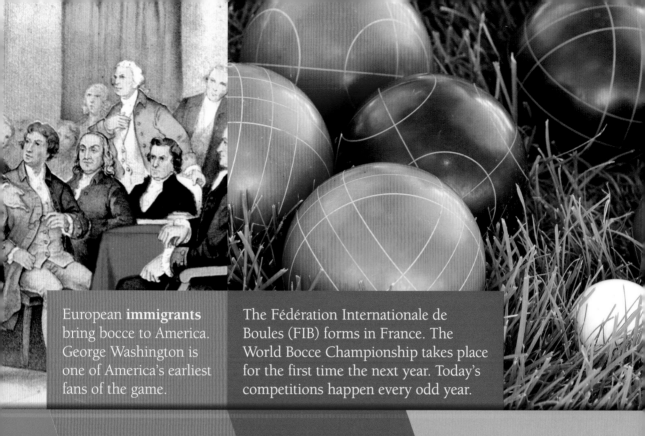

European **immigrants** bring bocce to America. George Washington is one of America's earliest fans of the game.

The Fédération Internationale de Boules (FIB) forms in France. The World Bocce Championship takes place for the first time the next year. Today's competitions happen every odd year.

18TH CENTURY

1946

2023

Berlin, Germany, will host the 2023 Special Olympics World Games. Bocce is an event at the this international competition.

What You Need

A set of balls and a flat area large enough to play in is all a person needs for a game of bocce. In the past, most bocce balls were handmade out of wood. Now, they are often made of a hard **composite material**. Ball sets are easily purchased in retail stores or online.

Competitive players may want extra equipment, such as carry bags, ball polish, measuring devices, and scoreboards, but these are luxuries. A pen, some paper, and household measuring tape are enough for a backyard game.

Bocce needs to be played on a flat surface so the balls do not roll away after they have been thrown.

Bocce Balls
Traditionally, bocce balls are simply called bocce, like the game. A set of bocce includes nine balls. There are usually four red, four green, and the pallino.

Scoreboard and Scorecards
Most scoreboards have a line of numbers, ranging from 1 to 12. Colored pins fit into small holes to mark teams' scores. Score cards are easy to print or draw if a scoreboard is not available.

Measuring Device
Sometimes, the distances between the balls and the pallino are not completely clear. Players can use a measuring tape or their hands and feet to figure out which ball is nearest.

Polish
A rough playing surface can scratch or scuff the balls. Polish smooths away scratches so that the balls roll properly.

The Court

Bocce games can take place wherever there is space and a smooth surface. Grassy areas and sandy beaches are very popular for casual games. Competitive games happen on a court.

A bocce court is rectangular in shape. Six-inch (15.2-centimeter) curbs keep the balls contained. The curbs are made of cement or wood for stability. Courts often have hard packed surfaces of fine sand, dust, clay, or even crushed seashells.

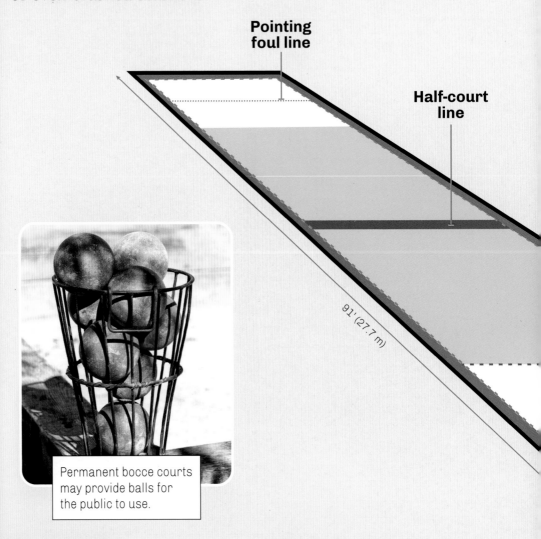

Pointing foul line

Half-court line

91' (27.7 m)

Permanent bocce courts may provide balls for the public to use.

For competitions, the United States Bocce Federation (USBF) recommends a court size that is 91 feet (27.7 meters) long and 13 feet (4 m) wide. Some families build bocce courts in their backyards. The average size of these courts is 60 feet (18.3 m) long and 12 feet (3.7 m) wide.

Backyard courts are normally smaller than the ones used in official games.

Court foul lines are for official bocce competitions. The pointing foul line marks where players can throw for points. Beyond this, there is a hitting foul line. Players must only hit the other team's balls beyond this line. At the start of each game, players must throw the pallino beyond the half-court line.

Inbound area of play

Hitting foul line

16' (4.9 m)

13' (4 m)

Rules of the Game

A game of bocce might have two, four, six, or eight players. They are always divided into two teams. The maximum number of players on a team is four.

Taking Turns

A coin toss decides the starting team. They throw the pallino and make the first shot. The other team then tries to get one of their balls closer to the pallino. Once they have done this or run out of balls, the first team resumes throwing their balls. Each time a team gets a ball closer to the pallino, the other team resumes play. This continues until both teams are out of balls.

Getting Points

Every ball that is closer to the pallino than the other team's closest ball gets one point. If only one ball is closer, that team gets one point. If all four balls are closer, they get four. In competitive games, players can also lose points by getting **penalties** for making illegal shots.

Score a Game

Only one team can score points each round. The game continues round-by-round until one team has scored 12 points. Some scoreboards go up to higher numbers. Teams agree on the winning score before the game begins.

Game Length

The length of the game depends on skill. The right shots mean players get more points and win faster. There are three techniques for throwing.

1 *Punto* is the gentle method of rolling the ball toward the pallino. Players must make this shot from behind the pointing line. They can grip the ball palm up or down.

2 *Raffa* is an aggressive method. The ball rolls faster and aims to knock either the pallino or an **opponent**'s ball into a different position.

3 *Volo* is an air shot. It tries to knock another ball away with a direct hit. Players need accurate aim for this shot.

A Game for All

Bocce was once a sport played mostly by men. In America, Italian social clubs and backyard events were the main places to play. Now, bocce is one of the most **inclusive** sports in the world. The low intensity game allows people of all ages and abilities to play and have fun.

About 25 million people play bocce in America alone. The game's popularity increased when women and children began to play. Aside from backyard family fun, bocce games occur at beachside picnics, park outings, and at recreation centers.

Metal balls are used in a French throwing version of the game called petanque.

Bocce is now the fastest-growing sport in the Special Olympics. It became a World Games sport in 1991, with 41 athletes competing. Four years later, that number of bocce competitors had more than tripled, with 151 athletes competing for the Special Olympics gold medal.

The Special Olympics version of bocce, called boccia, uses a chute.

Abu Dhabi hosted the 2019 Special Olympics World Games. A total of 290 countries and 7,000 athletes took part in a variety of events. It was the largest sporting and humanitarian event of the year.

All Day Long!

The longest bocce marathon EVER took place in Connecticut in 2019. It lasted for **33 hours** and **4 minutes**.

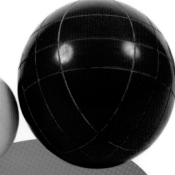

Winners!

The **Saudi Women's bocce team** won its **first-ever medal** in the **Abu Dhabi 2019 Special Olympics**.

Making It Big

While bocce has long been a leisure pursuit, it is now also an organized sport. Since 1947, the International Bocce Federation (FIB) has promoted and **regulated** the World Bocce Championships. Today, the organization includes more than 30 nations. Turkey was the host country for the 2019 World Bocce Championship.

In the United States, the official bocce organization is the United States Bocce Federation. Founded in 1977, it works toward promoting the sport and developing championship-level players. It also campaigns to have bocce included in the Olympic Games.

Bocce tournaments are held at purpose-built courts. That ensures each game is fair.

Umberto Granaglia

Umberto was born in Italy in 1931. He began playing bocce at five years old. By the age of 16, he was already winning tournaments.

In 1957, Umberto won his first world title championship. It was the start of a long winning streak. Twenty-three years later, he had won 13 World Championship titles, 12 European titles, and 46 Italian titles.

Umberto retired from bocce in the 1990s, but his legacy continues. No other bocce player has beaten his record. He became known as the "Player of the 20th Century."

Umberto passed away in 2008 at the age of 77.

Being a Good Sport

Good manners are always an important part of sports. The right attitude and behavior keep games fair and safe for everyone. Like other sports, bocce has its own **etiquette**. There are several unspoken rules that players follow to get along with others.

First, players should not distract others. They must be still and silent when it is not their turn. Second, players should be ready for their turn. The game gets too long when someone is slow to take shots. Third, players should not move the balls before or during scoring. As in other games, it is important for bocce players to accept defeat gracefully and not criticize others.

Spectators enjoying a game of bocce should watch quietly and not get in the way of the players.

If bocce games are played at night, good lighting is needed to make the games safe.

Bocce is a safe sport when people play safely. During backyard games, there may be other family members and pets around. Parked cars or houses can also be nearby. Players need to be aware of their surroundings. Bocce balls are hard. An improper throw could hurt someone.

Indoor and outdoor bocce courts are similar to bowling lanes. There are no nets or big dividers between courts. Following the rules is always the safest way to play.

A bocce ball has to be hard and heavy so that it does not bounce too much after it is thrown down the court.

A Healthy Game

While a bocce game is a great way to have fun, it can also help people stay healthy. Families usually play bocce outdoors on sunny days. Fresh air and sunshine make people feel better. Outdoors, the brain gets a good supply of oxygen. This improves focus and energy levels. Sunshine provides vitamin D to strengthen the **immune system**.

A fun game of bocce gets the whole body moving.

Playing bocce can increase flexibility and coordination over time. With a single shot, all areas of the body are active. Arms swing backward. Feet and legs move forward. The body bends, and the hand releases the ball. At the same time, the mind focuses on distances, speed, and direction.

Carrying a set of bocce balls can help develop muscle strength.

For some people, the social aspects of the game are most important. Being with others increases positive emotions and lowers stress. People feel happy and relaxed after a game of bocce. This improved state of mind can improve focus outside the game.

Big Game!

After soccer and golf, **bocce** is the **third** most popular **sport** in the world.

Healthy!

Hippocrates, a **Greek** doctor who lived from 460 to 375 BC, wrote about the **health benefits** of bocce.

Bocce Quiz

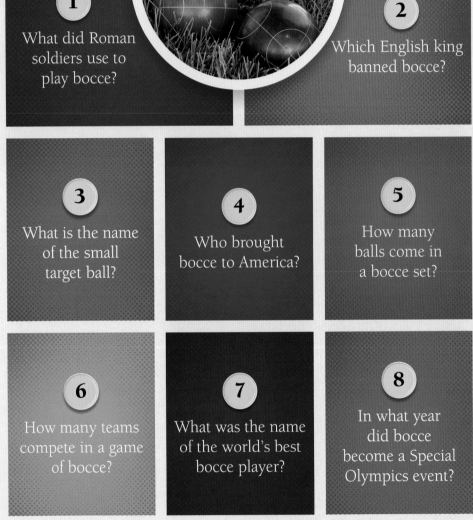

1
What did Roman soldiers use to play bocce?

2
Which English king banned bocce?

3
What is the name of the small target ball?

4
Who brought bocce to America?

5
How many balls come in a bocce set?

6
How many teams compete in a game of bocce?

7
What was the name of the world's best bocce player?

8
In what year did bocce become a Special Olympics event?

ANSWERS
1 Coconuts or round stones **2** King Henry VIII
3 The pallino **4** European immigrants **5** Nine
6 Two teams **7** Umberto Granaglia **8** 1991

Key Words

ban: to make an action or thing against the law

composite material: a material made by mixing other materials together, such as fiberglass or concrete

etiquette: a code of polite behavior belonging to a group

immigrants: people who come to live in a place from another country

immune system: the body's defense system against illness

inclusive: accepting of others

opponent: a person on an opposing team, or the opposing team

penalties: disadvantages placed on a team or athlete for breaking the rules

regulated: controlled by rules and observation

versions: styles of play that are similar

Index

Get the best of both worlds.

AV2 bridges the gap between print and digital.

The expandable resources toolbar enables quick access to content including **videos**, **audio**, **activities**, **weblinks**, **slideshows**, **quizzes**, and **key words**.

Animated videos make static images come alive.

Resource icons on each page help readers to further **explore key concepts**.

Published by Lightbox Learning
276 5th Avenue, Suite 704 #917
New York, NY 10001
Website: www.openlightbox.com

Library of Congress Cataloging-in-Publication Data

Names: Alaraj, Evangelene, author.
Title: Bocce / Evangelene Alaraj.
Description: New York : AV2, [2022] | Series: Backyard Games | Includes
  index. | Audience: Grades 2-3
Identifiers: LCCN 2021030398 (print) | LCCN 2021030399 (ebook) | ISBN
  9781791142230 (Library Binding) | ISBN 9781791142247 (Paperback) | ISBN
  9781791142254 (eBook)
Subjects: LCSH: Boccie (Game)--Juvenile literature.
Classification: LCC GV910.5.B63 A43 2022 (print) | LCC GV910.5.B63
  (ebook) | DDC 796.31--dc23
LC record available at https://lccn.loc.gov/2021030398
LC ebook record available at https://lccn.loc.gov/2021030399

Printed in Guangzhou, China
1 2 3 4 5 6 7 8 9 0 25 24 23 22 21

082021
101120

Project Coordinator Heather Kissock
Designer Terry Paulhus

Photo Credits
Every reasonable effort has been made to trace ownership and to obtain permission to reprint copyright material. The publisher would be pleased to have any errors or omissions brought to its attention so that they may be corrected in subsequent printings. AV2 acknowledges Getty Images, Alamy, Shutterstock, and Antonio Busso as its primary photo suppliers for this title.